Ben's New Trick

Written by Rachel Farber

Illustrated by Al Fiorentino

"When is Grandma coming?" said Ben.

"After ten," said Mom.

3

Then Ben ran out with Jen. Jen got up in the tree.

"Can I come up, too?" said Ben.

"No, not yet," said Jen. "But you can when you get big."

Ben ran back in. Dad was under the sink.

"Can I help you do that?" said Ben.

"No, not yet," said Dad. "But you can when you get big."

Then Ben ran to the den. Mom was painting in the den.

"Can I help you do that?" said Ben.

"No, not yet," said Mom. "But you can when you get big."

Then Ben heard Grandma. So he ran out.

"How is my big boy?" said Grandma.

"I'm okay," said Ben. "But Mom and Dad and Jen tell me I can't do things until I'm big."

"We can fix that," said Grandma.

"Grandma, Grandma," said Jen. "Do you have something for us?"

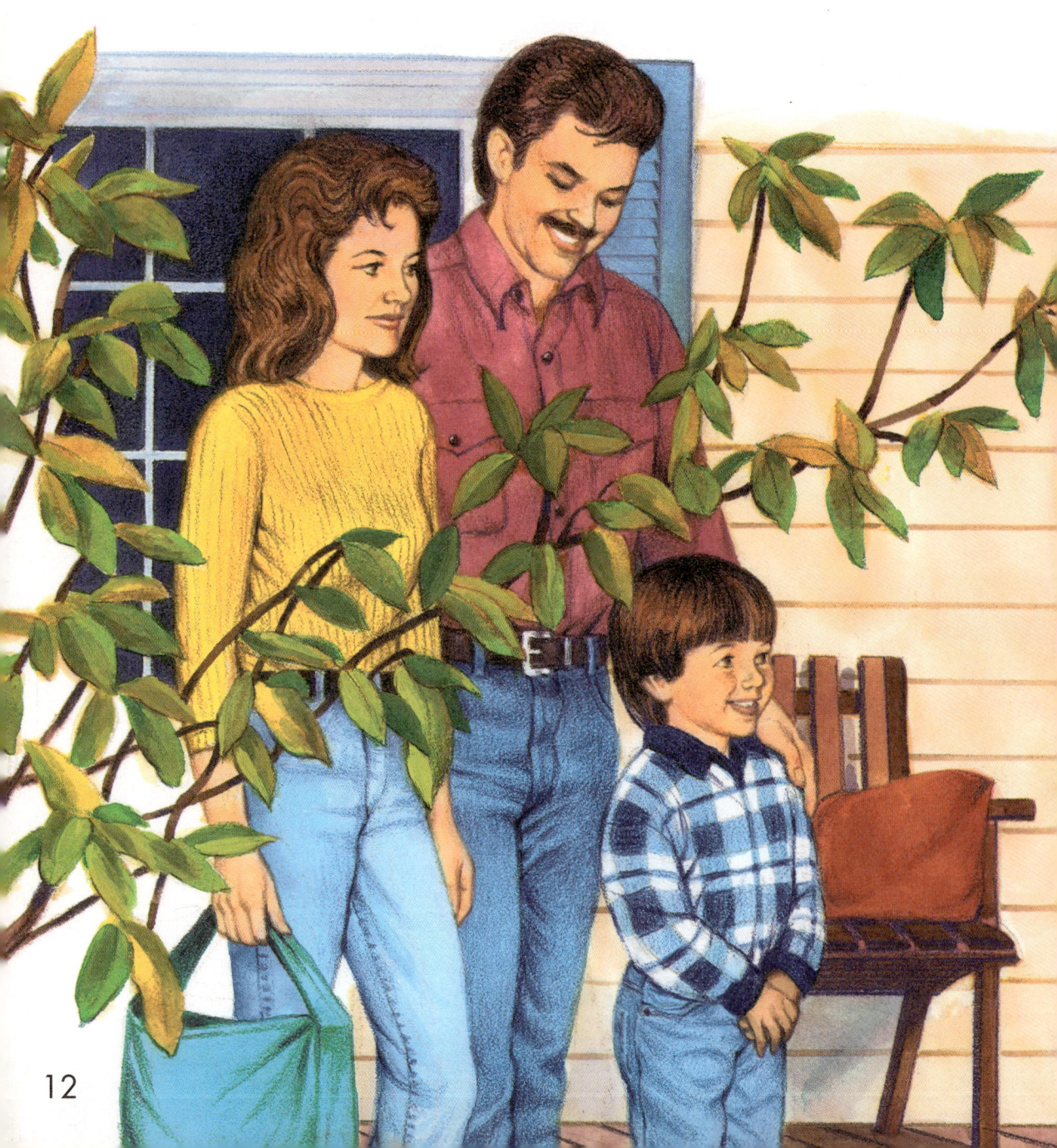

"Yes, I do," said Grandma. "I have a trick. The trick is to stand on one hand. Can you do it?"

"I bet I can!" said Jen.

But when she did it, she fell.

"I bet I'm too little," said Ben. "I can't do it until I'm big."

"No, no," said Grandma. "You can do it. Watch me."

"Look!" said Ben. "I can stand on one hand!"